# NFT Hand-Book for Beginners

*How to Make, Buy, Sell and Trade Non-Fungible Tokens to Make Money within No Time*

By

**Koala Publishers**
**Charles Murphy**

By reading this text, the reader accepts that the author will not be held liable for any damages, indirectly or directly, experienced due to the use of the information included herein, particularly, but not limited to, omissions, errors, or inaccuracies. As a reader, you are accountable for your decisions, actions, and consequences.

# About the Author

Charles Murphy is a Professor in Computer Science and Technology by profession. He has an eye for future technological trends as he is always eager to learn new things and share them with the audience. He has shown keen interest in the newest technological fields like Metaverse and Non-Fungible Tokens (NFTs) He is already investing in NFTs and coming up with his books to help the readers as much as possible. The best thing is that he always maintains the level of practicality in his books so that the readers come up with positive feedback after getting maximum learning. Along with a book on Metaverse Investment, he has also written a book on the value of NFTs and how they can be of any help for those who want to get greater profits in the said fields. He wants to share his expertise and deep knowledge with the readers so that they also jump into such a technological domain for earning profits.

# Table of contents

# Introduction

The world is moving forward rapidly, and technological development is the main reason. The business market is getting more competitive than ever, and the cutthroat economy makes business lives even more challenging. People keep looking for new and innovative ways to make money in such situations. Everyone is fully aware of the hype generated by cryptocurrency a few years back. People jumped into the industry in huge numbers and got their hands on huge profits.

However, the trends keep on changing, and if we talk about the present-day scenario, the Metaverse and Non-Fungible Tokens (NFTs) are making it to the news for all productive reasons.

Speaking of the NFTs, these tokens work on blockchain technology and are surely full of multiple profit prospects for people from different industries. In simple words, these tokens can be of different types, and people can buy or sell them to generate greater revenue. However, the actual domain of the NFTs is much bigger than this as it is already making it to the top-level industries.

It is possible to use NFT for money-making in several ways. Nevertheless, the best application is that NFTs are now being introduced in Blockchain-based gaming features. Several NFT games are available for the players that come with in-game collectibles. These in-game assets take the shape of NFTs, and the players will exchange them during the games.

Similarly, celebrities, artists, and even sports enthusiasts are also interested in the NFTs in the current days of 2022. Several singers and TV hosts have already launched their NFT collection, and their fans are busy buying these NFTs at huge costs. Snoop Dogg, for example, has the biggest NFT collection and is reportedly getting the biggest profit margins as well. The same goes true for the sports like Basketball and Football, where the players are coming up with specialized cards that take the name of NFTs. Many fans are ready to spend millions on these digital assets without even thinking twice.

A question may arise in your mind: Can a normal amateur person generate money through NFTs? The answer is simple: everyone can earn profits through NFTs until they follow all the required protocols. You can now make your NFT by digitalizing your artwork, a short video, or even a music file. The process of creating your own NFT is not rocket science anymore, as you will be able to do it quite easily by following the guidelines and instructions given in this book. Once you are done making your NFT, you will be able to sell it through a valid platform to target greater profits.

So, what are you thinking about? If you even have a minor interest in the NFT domain, now is the right time to dive in and learn about all the technical concepts. Read about the success stories of some top-ranked NFT projects that may convince you about the higher-level significance of the NFTs.

You may also go through the trends among the celebrities from late 2021 and early 2022 as for now that are already proving to be the kings of this particular domain. Wait no more and grasp all the concepts related to these non-fungible tokens. Give your art a form of NFT and try selling it for huge profits.

Last but not least, NFTs are already getting a huge hype in the present-day scenario. However, they will be even noisier in the years to come as the people are getting all the desired awareness related to the concept. So, before it's too late, you need to get into NFTs at the earliest and keep yourself updated about all the novel and innovative technological aspects.

# Chapter 1: NFTs & Metaverse

The hype surrounding non-fungible tokens has brushed the world and has become a foundation of a long debate. Nevertheless, one thing is sure: NFTs will play a vital part in forming a perfect metaverse. NFTs will open up new projections for investors, businesses, and fans in the long run.

NFTs have lately been utilized to make an entry or access to the metaverse. But what is the value of it to them? Is it critical for blockchain fanatics right now? Nevertheless, the projects, organized with public curiosity, will let NFTs and blockchain play a noteworthy role in the metaverse. It is a 3D digital world that offers users and enterprises an excess of options for transporting real-world goods and amenities. Using blockchain is likely to generate an open and reasonable economy. Because the gaming business has previously done what the metaverse aims to accomplish, the play-to-earn system will link the gap between NFTs and the metaverse, letting identity, public, and social interactions flourish.

## 1.1 NFTs with Huge Potential

Nearly every discussion in this business proposes that NFTs and the metaverse should be shared. We can see how these two are connected because of the quick development of blockchain gaming, powered by efforts to generate a virtual environment. Additionally, with NFTs, real-life characteristics and digital embodiments provide straight access to the metaverse.

NFT is known as a smart contract, a blockchain program that allows the network to reserve NFT contacts that can be retrieved later, which can help grow a metaverse economy in NFTs. NFT-based access can be the crucial focus at first to correctly gain access to the whole metaverse, such as VIP entry and so on. Compared to a subscription model, businesses might launch exclusive items or special access to content for followers. After that, NFTs will use location-based characteristics, interaction, and AR to offer interoperability outside the metaverse, leaving an efficient fan engagement behind. As we have progressively discovered, NFTs and the metaverse are connected in heaven.

Users and enterprises can now port real-world possessions and facilities into the metaverse, a decentralized virtual environment. Gaming models and blockchain games are an additional method to participate more real-world assets in the metaverse. The most renowned method for growing user engagement is the play-to-earn scheme. While they enjoy, players can also depend on NFTs and use in-game currencies. Additionally, unlike traditional gaming, these games are impartial because members will fully own their possessions rather than be controlled by a game.

It also underwrites to the rise in admiration of play-to-earn models and the metaverse as a whole. Guilds act as middlemen after buying in-game NFT possessions like land assets, which can then be shared with other players looking to make money in their distinct virtual worlds. On the other hand, these guilds take a small fraction of the earnings as fees. All of it leads to the formation of a Digital economy in which players who are incapable of paying money upfront can recruit the provision of guilds to kick-start their operation.

If you are aware of the modern digital art trends, you must have come across some information about them on the internet.

NFTs have been making headlines across the globe, from music to memes and everything in-between as collectors and investors contest for a piece of the action. This new technology seems to have fascinated the world with a series of high-profile sales.

In simple words, NFT is a tradable digital asset with a separate value from the rest of the collection's tokens. This is often a work of art kept in their cryptocurrency wallet's collectibles area to the buyers.

Irrespective of how you describe them, a handful of investors have relished noteworthy increases in their portfolios over the year 2021 as more people enter the marketplace with cash to spend.

Recognized firms have arrived at the industry to take benefit of the increasing trend as the digital art market endures to garner serious collectors' attention.

Suppose we talk about some of the most notable NFTs in the market in the current times of the early months of the year 2022, like Bored Ape Yacht Club, CryptoPunks, and Pudgy Penguins will be placed at the top of the list as they have lately surged in popularity. With current sales, each of these recent NFT enterprises has crushed the bank, surpassing the developers' and traders' expectations.

While traders with many Ethereum (ETH) are still attentive towards these collections, many investors are looking for new contestants to help them get the most out of their assets.

There are a few decent places to start looking for the next big NFT. And the best place to start is on social media. For example, you can just go through your Twitter feed as it is a hugely prevalent venue for promoting new work.

Nevertheless, following the Twitter feed isn't the only way to stay updated on new enterprises. Tracking sales has become a tried-and-true option for savvy traders to evaluate investors' mood as OpenSea and many other projects endure to increase its NFT collections. OpenSea features the most popular NFT collections obtainable and the chief volume of NFT sales in the game. Other names from the list include options like Rarible, SuperRare, Larva Labs, Nifty Gateway and NBA Top Shot.

In conclusion, if you have decided to enter into the NFT space, connecting a few Discord channels and heeding to the opinions of successful traders is a great idea. Before sales, these discussion forums are regularly used to build acceptance.

Speaking of the most popular NFT domains, the interested people can go with several options as far as the profit potentials are concerned. To start with, the digital art around us can always be converted into the NFTs of your choice. Moreover, the demand for art-based NFTs is growing at a rapid pace. It can be a short video, a perfect-looking painting, or even a photograph of a beautiful scene. All such things will be in huge demand almost all the time, and these will surely bring you a higher percentage of profits.

Moreover, an exciting and full of potential option in the NFT world is to buy virtual land at the desired location. Many Hollywood celebrities have already dived into this domain and generated huge profits. The digital land pieces are being given the shape of an NFT, and the buyers can place the auction prices as per the ongoing trends.

Last but not least, the sports industry is also engrossed in the NFT world to a certain extent. Most of the top athletes from sports like Basketball and Football are now coming up with their own NFTs, and their fans and followers are paying huge amounts of dollars for buying those. Some NFTs are also based on historic sports-related moments, like the most memorable NBA moments are already being given the shape of NFTs.

## 1.2 NFTs Worth Millions

The hype about crypto art has been making it to the news for over a decade, but NFTs have gained admiration with that outside of the blockchain technology mania in the year 2021. While traditional art has continuously been valued, NFTs are becoming a more popular means to trade digital art. Why would somebody pay almost as much for digital ownership of digital art as they would for a genuine piece of art? All of this hype is because they will get a real sense of ownership.

The scarcity of NFTs and the strong demand among the investors and the buyers have fueled a lot of attention towards these tokens. The CEO of Twitter, for example, has sold one for just around $3 million. As per reports, NFT sales totaled $300 million in the first two months of the year 2021 alone. Crypto art has carried in a lot of money for both creators and purchasers. In February 2021, Pablo Rodriguez from Miami resold a Beeple piece for roughly 1,000 times more than it had initially sold, demonstrating how lucrative the market can be.

According to Ivan Nefedkin, the CEO of Generative Gallery, the art market is developing, yet gallery holders have the same prospects as artists. We can completely transfer all of the elements of the art industry to the virtual format and complement them with completely new ones that come as a result of the latest technological developments.

People worldwide are lastly paying notice to a process going on for nearly two decades. Additionally, they are enthusiastic about paying for it in real money. Venue investors, collectors, and art-related companies have shown an augmented interest in this growing field.

Art collectors have been risking NFTs for a while and are now making investments in them with the expectation of growing their value and selling them for a profit.

According to Denis Belkevich, an economist from the art industry, the NFT market is gradually gaining traction among notable buyers and sellers. Many forecasters were doubtful about the NFT market in March 2021, especially after Beeple was sold for $69 million. The supply and demand ratio, on the other hand, suggests that the market has become more centralized, bringing a growing number of collectors to the NFT market. As per market data, NFT is becoming a common investment strategy, with short-term investments producing huge revenues in a shorter period.

# Chapter 2: Investing in NFT

The hype about NFTs and their investment potential is getting real, and the people are interested in them the most. All of us want to know what the NFTs offer today regarding their revenue-generating potential. If you want to dive into this competitive domain, now is the time to learn about all the technical aspects. To start with, you need to learn the art of buying, to sell, and creating an NFT to get access to huge profits.

## 2.1 Buying & Selling of NFT

People buy NFTs for a diversity of reasons. One of the most elementary reasons is that they wish to finance in a fresh, hypothetical, and highly volatile asset. In 2021, the market for NFTs reached its peak, and many NFT-based collections had their values skyrocket. CryptoPunk is the biggest example from the year 2021 as it gained the highest profit margins and the greatest popularity in this particular domain.

Some investors buy NFTs as a virtual art instead of gambling on their upcoming value. Many individuals wish to own infrequent, verifiably reliable digital art as the world advances more and more towards a virtual future in which we devote a lot of our communications and time online. Similar to the thought of a Metaverse, it continues to gain huge attention.

Others may buy an NFT as a gift for somebody they know would relish it, and so on. The causes diverge, but the fact is that the market has grown up to be noteworthy and should not be ignored.

Some people may consider spending huge dollars on PNG or GIF files illogical. Contrary to it, some people are still ready to pay a lot of money for something they could just view, screenshot, and download for free on the internet.

NFTs link social and financial capitals with each other while generating a huge network of connections among the representative community members. All the informative data on the blockchain is recorded efficiently and is verified by the already available verification mechanisms. It fundamentally helps the art creators to autograph their NFTs digitally while allowing the targeted customer base to get involved with the artists of the newly produced NFTs simultaneously. In short, using NFTs is the best way to upsurge your profit capital as far as the most organized and notable methods are concerned.

It does not matter if a picture or a music file has been shared multiple times online; the interested buyers can purchase an NFT because it is exclusive and uncommon. This should be the ultimate criterion for every serious art collector.

It is worth mentioning here that collectors are not procuring authentic content because they are not at all expected to hold the copyright. It is due to the technology that the content creator recalls the copyright, and the mainstream of NFT platforms lets them collect royalties when the product is traded again in the future.

As an alternative, while procuring NFTs, the potential buyers are receiving tokens that interlink their names to the art of the content creator on blockchain-based technology, which is the most appreciated thing right now.

By purchasing NFTs, collectors can obtain novel goods verified on the blockchain and serve as proof of ownership.

### Where to buy NFTs?

Buying a perfect NFT is not that difficult after all, and you can do it by going through a few notable platforms. The marketplace is getting bigger day by day, and you can come across a number of options to buy and sell the desired NFTs. All the platforms differ from each other to a certain extent as far as the buying mechanisms are concerned. Some notable names from the list include Nifty Gateway, Crypto.com and Binance.

Some other distinctions between different platforms can also be seen. For example, there may be a difference based on whether they accept the given NFT obligations, desired access, and the cost of making your own NFT. All such features should be considered by the buyers or the art creators while choosing a perfect marketplace.

Although each NFT platform operates contrarily, their mainstream provides a varied selection of NFTs to purchase. Contrary to this, experts of the domain select a platform based on the kind of non-fungible token they want to procure.

## Different Types of NFT Platforms

Speaking of multiple types of available marketplaces to buy NFTs, you may come across several different options. The first and the most important domain is the Mass Marketplaces, which are generally considered the bigger ones. The mass marketplaces refer to a bigger domain that consists of NFTs of different types, including art collections and in-game collectibles. OpenSea is the biggest and the most noteworthy example from the list of mass marketplaces.

You can also come across the curated marketplaces, as these are the places from where you will be able to buy the most exclusive sets of NFTs. Only those with a special eye for unique art pieces should be going towards these platforms. The most prevalent name from the domain of curated marketplaces is NiftyGateway.

Moreover, you can also go with the sports-based NFT platforms if you are interested in sports activities. Different players have launched their own NFTs. You can buy and sell these as well as have a go at the NFTs of the most memorable sporting events.

## Selecting a Crypto Wallet

After choosing a required collection, collectors must start registering an account on the desired platform to obtain NFTs. They will, nevertheless, need to link their cryptocurrency wallet to the selected NFT platform first, as they will not be able to buy or sell anything until then.

A crypto wallet helps secure storage for digital assets in any blockchain system. Associates of the crypto community need wallets to have access to blockchain applications, sign transactions and accomplish their balances conferring to blockchain essentials. All crypto platforms, chiefly NFT marketplaces, eradicate the need to keep user account data in this fashion, making their processes more accurate and safer.

Before getting a wallet, always ensure that it contests the cryptocurrency utilized on the platform the buyer will be using. Because the mainstream of NFT services is generated on the Ethereum platform, they take Ethereum's native cryptocurrency, Ether (ETH), as a type of payment. The options like Solana and Polka Dot are also considered noteworthy for the shopping of as many NFTs as you can. These currency options offer you a chance to buy the NFT of your choice by following the said mechanisms.

### Types of Wallets

Depending on their nature and work, digital wallets are generally divided into three main categories. All three of these are discussed below so that you may get an idea about the perfect wallet to choose from as per your requirements.

- **Hosted Wallet**

The most accessible and simple to set up a wallet is a hosted wallet. It is also known by the custodial name wallet. It is called so due to the fact that a third party routinely stores users' crypto in it, as compared to the way banks keep money in savings accounts. Users have nothing to be worried about with this type as third parties are accountable for the security of users' cryptocurrency.

The interested creators will never misplace their cryptocurrency even if they forget their password. The most noteworthy drawback of going with such a type is the loss of obscurity, as it regularly assists the users to undergo customer authentication, which refers to ID verification. Additionally, consumers must guarantee that the hosting firm is dependable and professional.

Some common wallet names that can help you in this regard are Metamask, Math Wallet, Alpha Wallet, Trust Wallet and Coinbase Wallet.

- **Non-Custodial Wallet**

It does not commend the security of its users' cryptocurrencies to a third party. In its place, it offers them eventual control over the security of their crypto money. Users don't have to make inquiries every time they want to convey cryptocurrency. Depending on how speedily they want a transaction to progress, they can choose between the default transaction charges and a higher fee.

Even though these wallets deliver the necessary software for keeping cryptocurrency, users are exclusively accountable for memorizing and protecting passwords. Users will not have to access their wallets if they forget their private keys. These wallets also let the creators complete advanced transactions such as lending, staking, borrowing, and more.

- **Hardware Wallet**

You may see it by the name cold wallet or Hardware wallet. Moreover, it is a small physical device similar to a USB drive. It is both challenging to use and expensive. The understandable advantage of having a hardware wallet is that users' private keys are firmly stored without the security issues linked with internet wallets. Even if the user's computer is hacked, this wallet can keep crypto money offline and secure them.

A perfect wallet depends on the collector's demands that mainly revolve around the level of security being offered by such different types of wallets. They can go with a hosted wallet to keep the acquisition process simple. On the other hand, a non-custodial wallet should be preferred to have comprehensive control over their crypto. Lastly, a hardware wallet is helpful in taking take extra precautions.

To recapitulate, after collectors have got their wallets and have adequate crypto funds, they may attach them to a suitable NFT marketplace, make an account, and start purchasing NFTs.

### Buying NFTs

You can now buy the desired NFTs in a number of ways, and almost all the processes are quite simple to understand. Even people with no previous knowledge can learn the art of buying the NFTs by going through the available material on the internet as there is no rocket science in the concept. The best option could be to buy the NFTs from the places that sell with the help of auctions. To be precise, the auction can be of two types; English and Dutch auction. The first one is a simple technique where the person with the highest bid will be considered as the winner, and he will be successful in getting his hands on the desired item.

On the other hand, the Dutch auction style is different to a certain extent. The price of the objects goes does as the auction goes along. Such a drop in the price is specific in nature, and the buyers need to follow the trends. All it requires is a perfect moment to buy a perfect NFT at a reasonable price. All you need is a chance to be present there at the time of the price drop.

If you are not interested in buying from the auction, you can go with a third option as well. Now is the time to complete the remaining steps and close the deal. On every buying platform, you will see a button that denotes the option of BUY NOW on the platforms like OpenSea, Binance, Crypto.com, Nifty Gateway and GameStop. Locate it and click it to progress through the process of buying an NFT. Such sites display the NFTs at fixed prices. You will be able to save a lot of time as well as money in some cases, and you will be saved from all the headaches and disturbance during an online auction. However, when you plan to buy through such a platform, make sure you see the price of the NFT with open eyes. Move your attention to the type of currency for the price. It can be in dollars, or it can be in the ETH format or the currencies like Solana and Polka Dot.

### Selling NFTs

There are two chief ways to sell NFTs: selling a newly minted NFT that is the preferred method for content creators and trading an NFT that a collector has previously purchased and is ready to trade.

The NFT creation or minting process is expected to finish in two ways. Minting is a simple method by which content such as works of art, music, collectibles, and other novel items become a blockchain. The content transforms into an NFT and is instantly tokenized. Since then, these virtual things have been able to be sold and traded as NFTs and virtually traced when re-sold.

Content creators will just require a personal computer, a crypto wallet that provisions NFTs, and an account on a blockchain-focused NFT marketplace to start minting.

Additionally, while selling NFTs, NFT markets may ask content providers to select a royalty rate. When the NFT is sold to a new buyer, royalties earn a specific commission. Due to the basics of non-fungible tokens' technology, royalties can provide enduring passive income streams for creators.

Furthermore, the mainstream of NFT exchanges offers the option of choosing a selling method or fixing a price for the NFT while minting a token. As a result, freshly minted NFTs are regularly thought to be put up for sale soon after they are created.

In other conditions, art creators must log in to their NFT marketplace accounts and find the digital objects from their NFT collections to sell them. They should click on the required NFT pieces after they have sited them.

The chief distinction is that when NFTs from a provisional collection are sold, collectors will not gain royalties. Royalties in the form of percentages of any future sales will be transported straight to the wallets or original developers of the NFTs.

Consequently, creators are persistently linked to copyright on their creative output in the form of NFTs, while they only acquire NFTs in their collections for a limited time. Collectors of NFTs, similar to collectors in other traditional markets, have only negligible ownership rights, such as the right to hold and sell, and these rights expire when the NFT is sold.

Despite the unpredictability and immature nature of the crypto market as a whole, as well as the high amount of vagueness surrounding their prices, the NFTs revolution continues to spread. Buying NFTs is still a fanciful way to help artists, designers, singers, and other creative people where collectors are concerned about such digital assets.

## 2.2 Creating your Own NFT

Now that you are done reading about how to buy and sell an NFT, now is the time to focus your attention on the question of whether you can make your own NFT or not. What will happen if you are successful in creating your non-fungible token. The bonus feature is that you will be the sole owner, and you will be able to sell it to anyone who pays the highest price. The process of creating your own NFT is not that difficult after all. Try to remember a few basic steps, and you will be all ready to come up with your personal NFT.

### Pick your Item

The most important thing you must do is select the artwork. Non-fungible tokens can characterize any digital file. A digital painting, a music tone, a text, or a movie can all be transformed into NFTs. Anything that can be kept as a multimedia file qualifies the required criteria. After all, the NFT game aims to turn digital artwork into dynamic items in an age of unlimited reproduction.

### Bring Some ETH, Solana, or Polka Dot

Now is the time to get some ETH or other notable currencies like Solana or Polka Dot in your wallet if you select a perfect piece of digital art that you want to convert to an NFT. Minting an NFT will likely be costly. Consequently, you will need an Ethereum wallet with some Ether in it. For this purpose, you can go with Metamask as it is the easiest to use. However, you can also consider some other wallet options like Alpha Wallet, Math Wallet, Coinbase Wallet and Trust Wallet. Let's consider Metamask as it is a free application that you may get on your iPhone or Android phone. The price required for the NFT is quite adjustable. As per the year 2022, you should have at least $100-150 in Ether, but remember that the minting process could charge you much more depending on the daily operative price.

**Select a Selling Platform**

After having everything in place, you just need to select a marketplace where you will generate and then list your NFT. Rarible, Mintable, and OpenSea are the most prevalent options. You do not need to be a verified artist to sell on the marketplace. But, this also means that the marketplace is overflowing with digital trinkets that no one will ever buy.

In simple words, go to the OpenSea platform or any other platform of your choice and click on the option named "My Profile." You can pick how to continue with linking your ETH wallet on this page. The method is rather easy to follow.

**Creation of NFT**

You can now shape your first NFT after linking your ETH wallet to OpenSea. Generate a collection by selecting "Create" from the top menu. Fill in all of the compulsory information, then save. You are now prepared to start the actual minting of a new NFT. Select "New Item," upload your art and write as many particulars as you wish. Click "Create" when you are all ready to have your NFT.

**Advertise Properly**

So, you have made an NFT and effectively listed it on the OpenSea marketplace. Waiting for someone to have a look at your valued token is not going to get you very far. You will have to promote the object yourself, and to a pre-existing group of people concerned about your work. That's the hardest part, and it has nothing to do with the creative process. It is just as ruthless and particular as the kingdom of actual art. However, this is the only way to give your best to attract maximum buyers towards your digital assets.

**Can I Sell my NFT?**

If we go by a one-word answer, the reply will be Yes; you can surely sell your own NFT. You simply have to follow the instructions after successfully developing an NFT. The first thing is to set up your NFT for an auction. As previously discussed, you can go with the English or Dutch method of the auction that will decide the final selling price of your NFT. The price also depends on the ongoing trends. If your NFT is as per the modern trends and demands, you will be able to sell it in no time.

The next step is to write a detailed description of your NFT so that the people are clear enough about its significance and properties. You have to upload the NFT details on the platform you selected to sell your non-fungible token. You can go with as many details as you want to end up convincing a maximum number of buyers.

Lastly, while uploading your NFT to the desired platform, you will be needed to pay the listing price. Now you are in a position to fight for the selling competition. No matter which NFT domain you have chosen, the chances are higher that you will face strict competition in almost all cases. Only the unique and the most exclusive NFTs will be getting the highest attention in such situations.

# Chapter 3: NFTs & Revenue Generation

The main reason behind the growing acceptance of NFTs all around the globe is their profit producing potential. It has been made possible in a number of ways and the interested individuals can jump in to learn about all the potential possibilities. The most notable domains include NFT-based games and buying a virtual piece of land in a virtual land. Apart from that, you can also come across various other possibilities.

## 3.1 Play & Earn Gaming Features

The popularity and hype of NFT-based games are on a regular rise and people are getting in this domain more than ever as per the trends of late 2021 and early 2022. Apart from entertainment, it is directly helpful in earning you a lot of money.

You should have a clear understanding now that NFTs are digital assets based on blockchain technology. This attribute makes them flawless for usage as consumables, characters, and other tradeable possessions in video games.

In the game-fi world, NFT games have gone prevalent to make money. You can sell your in-game NFTs to other players. Another idea is to use play-to-earn models to gain as many tokens as you can.

Always keep your gaming NFTs in a wallet that accepts them. When you send an NFT to a marketplace or another user, make sure you keep a closer look at the potential frauds. Lastly, check the guidelines of every NFT game you play cautiously to learn if there is any risk of losing.

The mainstream of NFT games may be found on Ethereum and the Binance Smart Chain. Some hire collectible characters like Axie Infinity & CryptoBlades in their battles, while some may go for collectible cards like Sorare.

Binance also sells some Mystery Boxes based on the NFTs, which permit users to own NFTs of numerous rarities. These Boxes are part of the possessions that feature NFT games.

These games have progressed to offer play-to-earn models since they were first launched with the CryptoKitties domain. Such a domain syndicates the worlds of finance and gaming, letting users earn money as they play. You will not have to depend on your luck to win or breed a rare asset worth thousands of dollars.

Such games are not similar to merely keeping crypto-collectibles in your wallet. NFTs will be used in the mechanisms, rules and player connections of an NFT game. For example, a game might use an NFT to characterize your exclusive avatar or character. You can also link NFTs to digital things while playing the game. You can then swap or trade your NFTs for revenue with other gamers. The added bonus is that you can generate money from NFT games using an entirely new domain, a play-to-earn paradigm that makes it to the news for all productive reasons.

So, how do you precisely include NFTs in a gaming environment? Developers shape smart agreements that make up the guidelines for the NFTs used in a game to produce, exchange and implement them. On a blockchain, smart contracts are self-executing bits of code.

If we take the example of CryptoKitties, it is organized by a small number of core contracts. Originally, the game's code was kept under wraps. Players who were attracted even developed algorithms to calculate the chances of exact cat features showing up. Players could utilize this info to recover their chances of creating a valued rare breed.

The NFT-based games with the play-to-earn feature let players make money while they have entertainment at the same time. A player is frequently bestowed with tokens and, on occasional sessions. These tokens are the NFTs that own sole importance in such gaming features. It works on the principle that the longer you play, the more you earn. The tokens you obtain are regularly required in the game's creating process.

The token method is frequently more dependable because tokens can be added constantly through gameplay, whereas NFT drops are more arbitrary. Users coming from underprivileged nations have gathered to get the best out of the play-to-earn games as a substitute or complement to fixed income or communal security.

One of the most renowned games from this particular domain is Axie Infinity. You should either make a preliminary investment of three Axies or get a free bonus from an additional participant to participate in the game. You can also get your hands on the ERC-20 token that can be traded on interactions after you have a Team of your own and start achieving the given tasks and challenges.

Breeders utilize these tokens to generate new Axies, ensuing a huge market for the item. Axie Infinity also raised acceptance in many Asian countries, where many interested players started to depend on its play-to-earn tactic to make ends meet. The average earning of such players is somewhere between (200-1000) $ per month as per the analysis of the year 2021-22, with some receiving much more due to favorable market conditions and the total invested time.

## NFTs in Blockchain Games

The concept of NFTs is not new anymore and they took the gaming world by storm back in 2021. As for the year 2022, it will unquestionably become one of the most modern subjects in various industries. Are you still confused about the interest of the gaming world in blockchain-based technology? Do you think it will be beneficial enough for the players or not? You need not worry as you will be getting answers to all such queries soon enough.

All of you must have a clear idea about the meaning and significance of an NFT, irrespective of whether it is working in gaming or not. The name makes it sound classy, but the actual concept is even more simple than your expectations. An NFT is a digital good's documentation of ownership that is intended to be formed in a limited number.

Big organizations, mostly in the gaming industry, favor NFTs to produce a steady stream of cash from digital material. If an exclusive Fortnite skin is provided as an NFT, a player might be the first to unlock it in-game and then claim possession of it. After that, the skin's token can be sold back to the highest bidder, for a large sum of money. Irrespective of how much the skin sells for, Epic Games will take a share of the profit, and the new owner can resell it to other players indefinitely, with Epic taking a specific share on every sale.

Apart from introducing NFT perceptions to any game that bids cosmetic skins, it is also easy to see how they could be functional to card-collecting games. Such a feature can also be seen in the EA Sports' Ultimate Team modes. Every card in such a gaming approach could fundamentally be its own NFT, and you could then auction off ownership of any card in your deck to other players, with Electronic Arts getting a fraction of the auctioned sales.

Apart from getting a specific share when a player buys a pack of cards, the EA and other gaming companies can solely make the revenue based on the card sales until the NFTs are feasible enough.

Even though none of the instances described above have occurred yet, anyone with even a transitory interest in the games business can see where this journey is headed. NFTs are now the centre of attention to big game developers as they open up the chance of making a lot of profit on rare things. New trends like time-limited essentials have previously become the norm, but what if the game providers could only trade a precise number of cards? The call for those things would soar, resulting in a lively market.

NFTs can become the next step in the development of in-game microtransactions. This idea has advanced from battle passes to loot boxes and the concept is moving forward in the best possible manner.

Is it likely for a game provider to generate its own auction house without trusting the blockchain? NFTs, on the other hand, are an exclusive beast as they mix enduring cash flow with current investor interest in blockchain technology. Companies will be eager to pick the NFT way if it allows them to attract investors while still making money.

You need not get too far on the internet to determine passionate influences for and against NFTs. Yet, the enthusiasm of the discussion can make it seem as if pieces of evidence and realities are being overlooked at times. Arguments contradicting NFTs commonly mention environmental apprehensions and cryptocurrency questions, which aren't always pertinent to all NFTs.

The introduction of blockchain is the main modification between an NFT and the type of downloadable content that we have been trading in games for years.

When you currently procure a skin or avatar in a game, it is connected with an account. It might be an account for a specific game or a larger version that you use for all Ubisoft games. The game provider has complete control over how Downloadable Content (DLC) functions, counting how it validates your ownership, the server with which you download it, and how such pieces are merged in the game. Depending on the coding process, the way skin or a health potion is shown in one game may entirely be diverse in another.

## Top NFT-Based Games

Since their commencement, NFTs have repeatedly demonstrated that they have the aptitude to renovate the gaming industry. The growth of NFTs brings an innovative and exhilarating era in which online gamers take on even more significant roles in the gaming economy and are given rewards and compensations accordingly. Today, as game makers progressively incorporate blockchain technology to make their games even more thrilling, this gaming model is beginning to take shape.

Some specific platforms have placed themselves as the chief highpoint of the NFT gaming market, as they have in all the established sectors. Because they have effectually blended NFTs with prevalent game domains, these games are at the forefront of the existing NFT craze. Consequently, players can relish some of their preferred game genres while also contributing to a profitable NFT market. Read about the most prominent names from the NFT-based gaming industry.

## Axie Infinity

It takes motivation from the Pokemon game franchise and incorporates a blockchain rotation to make the ultimate product even more captivating. Players collect and breed NFT-based virtual pets called Axies in this game with the chief goal of battling other players. Each Axie comes with its exclusive genetic signature. These virtual creatures, as predictable, can be exchanged on Ethereum NFT platforms. Moreover, the final prices vary depending on their exclusiveness and distinctive characteristics.

To begin playing the game, you have to collect three Axies. To be precise, its native currency is known as Smooth Love Potion and SLP. It is bestowed for each mission, combat, and adventure mode you complete. You should pay a certain amount of SLPs for each contest to breed a new Axie, which you can also procure during the exchanges. ASX serves as the game's governance token and is another ERC20 token specifically associated with Axie Infinity.

## Sandbox

It is one of the most prevalent NFT games, even though it is more of a formation platform than a game. Consider it to be an NFT-powered Minecraft where you can both have fun while playing and create games and more exciting content on your own. Only in this game can you own your formations and trade them using the SAND token on the internal marketplace.

The game mode is another side of Sandbox, where you can generate your universe by adding games and happenings and producing a metaverse within The Sandbox. You may have fun while going to the games, discover other people's worlds, and import content into your collection. It is handled by LAND token and permits players to vote on new features.

The gaming visuals are amicable and meaningful to Minecraft, but there's much more you can do with it. It is captivating to see plots intermingling with other users from different countries. Like The Walking Dead, some top-ranked companies are in line to get linked with such gaming options.

## Sorare

It is a game based on NFT and Fantasy Football. This is a must for you if you are interested in real football matches. It links the fantasy gaming concepts into weekly tournaments in which the real-world happenings of the world's top football leagues will ultimately influence your pack of cards.

You can now have your footballer cards and create a pack of as many as five sports heroes to participate in weekly tournaments. Like other fantasy football, how these footballers perform during the week will finally impact your point total. Some of the most popular clubs included in this domain are Bayern Munich, Liverpool, and Bayern Munich.

## Battle Racers

It is influenced by the popular game Super Mario Kart as evident from the name. The ultimate aim is to mix numerous weaponries. It should result in some of the highly powered automobiles. Players can mix and match numerous pieces to benefit from the arcade-style tracks. You can record your valued or winning cars as NFTs on the blockchain and then trade them for cryptocurrency on OpenSea.

Each player has a clear aim to build the decisive car by prioritizing various aptitudes and characteristics. Having an aim to win maximum tournaments, you could prioritize speed and thrill over handling or comfort. This game is currently obtainable to play on Decentraland.

**Champions of National Football League**

Assuming NFT Champions to be a blockchain-based battle and an adventure game, if you have any know-how about the Pokemon game, you must have already figured out the working mechanism.

It offers story-driven gameplay with diverse projects for players to achieve, assuring that each player has exclusive gaming knowledge. The game explains through numerous locations, each with its champions and objectives.

The ultimate aim is to finalize a squad of occasional and influential monsters known as Champions. Each Champion is signified on the blockchain as an NFT, which can be changed into more commanding forms with an extensive variety of features and attack abilities.

## 3.2 Buying Virtual Land

NFT virtual land is an ownable territory of digital land on a metaverse platform. Decentraland, Axie Infinity and The Sandbox are the most prevalent NFT land developments. It is because each NFT is exclusive. They are well-suited to articulating land possession. They also make it unpretentious to show virtual ownership. NFT land can be utilized for various purposes, including publicity, socialization, gaming, and work.

In many cases, the property-owners can utilize their plot to host online experiences, demonstrate different types of talent or receive multiple gaming perks. Multinational companies and celebrities, such as Snoop Dogg and Adidas, have already invested in NFT land.

The utility and market conjecture all affect the value of the land. NFT land can be acquired directly from a scheme or on the secondary market via an NFT exchange like Binance NFT Marketplace or OpenSea. Just before you complete the purchasing deal, make sure you comprehend the dangers and possible uses of the land and the project it is elaborated with.

The development of Metaverse has deposited a batch of new blockchain applications. It is no astonishment that virtual land has developed a protruding issue since 2020 was such a huge year for the Metaverse and NFTs.

Other NFT land auctions have attained prices that are more advanced than those of physical belongings, making the insight problematic to measure for some. There are many counterparts between NFT land and old-style real estate. Nevertheless, being a blockchain-based digital asset, NFT land has separate features to examine.

Metaverse projects, as beforehand stated, are virtual surroundings that players can discover using 3D avatars for conferences, concerts, and explanations. For instance, SecondLive offers regions and venues. While some metaverse platforms do not permit users to procure a perpetual VR place, others do it regularly. To offer on the market, developers produce huge maps of land detached into small chunks.

Users obtain NFTs tangled to a specific plot of land to symbolize the area's sole ownership. These plots are obtainable for acquisition straight from the projector on the secondary market. What you can achieve with NFT land differs depending on the project.

Well-known superstars and companies have previously purchased land in the Metaverse. On The Sandbox, for example, Snoop Dogg is creating his Metaverse. Adidas has also acquired metaverse space on the platform. Apart from implementation in the metaverse and NFT craze, brands and businesses will offer users the prospect to interrelate with them through metaverse facilities and games.

**How to Buy Virtual Land?**

To start with, you need to select the right type of seller and confirm the platform's authenticity to save yourself from any fraud. You should be going with a reputable source so that you do not end up wasting your money. Make sure you never transfer something to the wallet of the seller. Prefer closing the deal with the help of third-party platforms like OpenSea or Binance Marketplace.

The next step is to decide whether you plan to sell it for a profit or you will be renting it to some other interested people. The final price of the land will depend on the purpose you want to fulfill after buying a virtual piece of land. In addition, the price also depends on the total traffic on your desired plot.

For buying, you should have an account on a reputable platform. After that, you will need currency in your wallet. Most of the time, you can get the deal done with the help of ETH. After you select the platform and have enough currency in your wallet, you can go on to the "Buy Now" option to close the deal.

Always remember to select the NFT-based virtual plots carefully. Not every project guarantees success in this particular domain. So, if you want results as per your desires, you should be spending a lot of time on the selection process. It can also be done with the help of going through the modern trends and the popularity level of a specific project.

In short, to complete the buying process of a virtual land plot, you should connect your wallet with your account on the buying platform. Decentraland enjoys a sound reputation in this regard. You can also prefer any other option as per your needs. Fill your wallet with the relevant currency, select your favored piece of digital land and close the deal.

## How to Make Money on Virtual Land?

### Rent it Out

Landowners can now rent out their land to others, such as game providers, huge studios, artists, who don't have sufficient money to buy virtual land or didn't get an option to do so throughout the early auctions. The land is rare in virtual blockchain platforms, especially in key places. Once all of the major real estates has been traded, the demand for land for rent will rise steeply.

By renting out your virtual land, you offer other people the chance to run businesses in the virtual world while also making a monthly rent. You can ask for rent by giving it out as a blank space, letting your occupants start their enterprise on it. On the other hand, you can construct whatever you want, such as an art gallery, empty building, hotel, or even a restaurant and rent out the place to certain companies.

## Make a Virtual Company

You can shape your own business and sell virtual merchandise on your virtual land. There is a diversity of businesses you can begin to earn money. You could also start a store to sell virtual attire and other products. You may open an office or a shop, hire your staff and activate a successful business.

## Organize Gatherings

You may throw parties on your land and charge real money from the people to allow them entry for the events like live shows, virtual concerts, themed parties, and other events. It will turn out to be progressively popular in the time to come, and you may take benefit of this trend by opening a venue of your own. You can become a host for the events yourself or rent out your place for huge charges to others who want to conduct their own events.

## Advertisement Spots

Any real-world action, including publicity, can be simulated in virtual blockchain kingdoms. You may develop your land as per the trends and transform it into the most private and stimulating publicity space possible. Some firms, such as virtual real estate owners or game developers, may be attracted to purchasing advertising space on your land. However, all of it will surely depend on the location of the virtual land.

## Self-Promotions

You can utilize your virtual land to widen your influence, whether you are a corporate owner or an art seller or a service provider of any type. This trend is getting immense publicity nowadays and a large number.

**Buy & Sell**

Procuring virtual blockchain lands and then vending them for a turnover is the simplest way to benefit from your virtual land. It will be even more helpful, especially if your land is attractive enough for huge traffic. Holding onto your land while it rises in value may be a perfect option if you are persistent. You might be able to earn more money this way.

## 3.3 Selling your Art in Terms of NFT

NFTs have lately been extensively used for trading virtual artworks through online markets such as SuperRare and Nifty Gateway. Digital artists regularly confront noteworthy exclusive rights issues: unlike drawings or hand-made sculptures, their work can be imitated and used indefinitely and without approval, letting down its value. However, artists can now attach their digital work to an NFT, letting it be genuine using the token's exclusive code. Blockchain-based technology archives every contract and the artwork's holder can verify ownership and shelter it from hackers. If the owner's account is hacked, stealing can still occur, but it will be tougher.

Many collectors and artists believe that NFTs can revolutionize the virtual fine art market. As you may be aware, lately, an auction house sold a collection of NFT artworks by Beeple for around €58 million. Purchasers hope that, like any other abstract asset, the NFT art market will flourish, growing the value of their preliminary investment. Some worry, nevertheless, that the NFT market may quickly devalue and crash, leaving new investors high and dry.

There has also been news of NFTs mysteriously vanishing after purchase, representing potential defects in the new technology. NFTs have also increased considerably over the environmental influence of digital products, together with the crypto with which they are accepted and sold.

These are, nevertheless, captivating times for young digital artists. Digital art has been infamously tough to the mint for years, but there is now a whole new platform for it. Even better for the artists, NFTs include a popular royalty feature, in which the art provider is paid a fee each time one of his works is sold.

To start, make up your wallet and deposit some Ethereum into it. This will support you in taking care of your gas expenses.

After that, you will want to circumnavigate to your favored NFT platform. You will need to make an account and interlink your wallet to it. It is worthwhile to pick your NFT platform first, then look into which wallets are supported. Nevertheless, if you are already using a well-known wallet, you should not have any difficulties.

This is when things start to get thought-provoking. You will have to submit your NFT. Most organizations permit you to upload a single NFT or multiple NFTs at once. On specific platforms, uploading many files is mentioned as a collection.

Whether you upload a single file or multiple art types, you will need to fill out the NFT's basic info. Relying on the platform, you may need to put up a sale or just specify the price you wish for your piece of art.

Lastly, if you choose to put money into something, you will have to pay for gas. After you have completed that, you may build your item and share it with the rest of the world. This is everything that you need to do with your artwork.

It is essentially quite modest to sell an NFT. Some platforms simplify for artists to progress and sell NFTs in a few simple steps. The word artist is emphasized because many individuals feel that making NFTs out of anything will result in sales, but this is not the case. Productive NFT artists have a long-term project with a solid track record to back up their releases. Advertising techniques and the promotion of their work are equally crucial.

In short, the process of making and selling an art-based NFT is not that difficult after all. You may have read about the basic steps quite several times. The fact that is even more important is that success will depend on the nature of your art and NFT.

On the other hand, if you go with any random piece of art and convert it into an NFT, you may not come across huge sales. Therefore, it is extremely important to know about the latest trends from the art world. It will help you go towards the right type of artwork so that you may get some eye-catching profits.

# Chapter 4: Significance of NFTs

It has been noticed that the popularity of NFTs is growing with each passing day. If we look around the internet, we will come across a number of successful projects linked with the NFTs that are bringing huge revenues for the companies, celebrities and even the common people from all around the world. Before you jump in the NFT world and plan to cement your place, you should be interested in grasping all the information about all the potential growth of this domain.

## 4.1 Success Stories of NFT Projects

NFTs came to the scene for the first time in the year 2021. All the crypto fanatics and investors are interested in this domain now more than ever to get a piece of the action. Do you have any idea about their potential significance? Do you know the main reasons behind their growth potential? What do you consider is the most influential reason behind the growing trends of using NFTs among celebrities? You will get to know the answers to all these questions just below.

NFTs run on Ethereum and other blockchains using smart contracts. They can be utilized to allocate assets and use the blockchain to verify their legality.

NFTs were first anticipated in 2015, with the first projects reaching the pipelines in 2017. Exclusive things like rare collectibles are being traded online using non-fungible token enterprises. Because each token is dynamic and cannot be replicated, NFTs generate scarcity, making them striking to collectors, vendors and artists. They are being bought and traded at auctions, with ETH and bitcoin as payment BTC.

NFTs have an optimistic future in the speedily emerging field of decentralized finance. They can be utilized to get loans with valuable assets like rare antiques, art samples and real estate, stocks, bonds and much more.

## Noteworthy Projects

A number of billionaires have entered the domain due to the bitcoin development, and they are searching for other virtual assets to capitalize on their earnings. The most productive NFT initiatives in 2021 are typically those that sell exclusive and limited-edition things, such as music, digital art and virtual assets at the most exorbitant costs. Speaking of one of the most precious NFTs ever sold, Beeple traded one in the year 2021 for $69 million at Christie's after a series of NFT auctions of virtual artworks.

Now is the time to discuss some more notable names from the NFT industry that are already making it to the news.

## Axie Infinty

It is an NFT-based game that produces a character named Axie. It works on the Metaverse principles and is already a lot of excitement. It has swiftly got to the top of the most popular NFTs. It comes with a play-to-earn feature where the players will be able to make a lot of money while having entertainment at the same time. It was launched in the year 2018. Axies are the in-game NFTs that players may exchange for a profit with some other players.

## CryptoPunks

It is a collection of thousands of software-generated punk-style figures and was launched in 2017. Each punk has its character and distinctive characteristics that say a lot about its collector value. The collection's unveiling assisted in the ERC-721 standard for NFTs on the blockchain, which now helps as the basis for the NFT market. The most valued CryptoPunk was being sold for 124,457 ethers, which was esteemed around $532 million at that particular time.

## Art Block

It is a collection of multiple artworks formed by varied artists using a smart contract on the Ethereum-based blockchain. The different types within the script that produce the art are available in the ERC-721 NFTs. The photos are available in both 2D and 3D formats. Such photos are rare art pieces and are being sold at huge prices. As per authentic research, some of these are even being sold at a price as huge as $6.5 million.

## Bored Ape Yacht Club

The unique club we are going to talk about started in April 2021. It is a collection of almost 10,000 ape characters. These apes vary based on color, facial signs, expressions and the accessories they wear from time to time. These were introduced with some new features to keep NFT owners involved. One category is also known by Bored Ape Kennel Club, which assists ape holders in adopting a dog-based NFT, which allows holders to mint Mutant Ape NFTs. NFTs from this club and Mutant Ape can also be traded on NFT exchanges.

## NBA Top Shot

This one is a perfect success story for sports enthusiasts as the National Basketball Association (NBA) connected with Dapper Labs, a developing company. The NBA Top Shot is a collection of some of the most memorable video clips of crucial moments from NBA games. These short videos are being given the shape of NFTs and the interested members can trade these for huge profits. It is one of the most successful NFT projects as it has already recorded more than 10.8 million transactions.

## Mutant Ape Yacht Club

Having the total sales worth $416 million compared to those for the original Bored Ape collection, it is an NFTs coin collection. Over the year 2021, it has established a huge market on its own. It comprises 20,000 Mutant Apes, which can only be made by revealing a Bored Ape to get your hands on the bottle of mutant serum.

## Loot for Adventurers

It is a collection of multiple text descriptions. These are for the objects in role-playing games with a total of almost 8000 NFTs available at the platform. A new community is being formed, with dynamic guides, generative network, artwork, and multiple other possessions. Other projects are in the development phase to create supplies, animals and numerous other things.

## Meebit

Larva labs launched it in May 2021. An algorithm produced 20,000 three-dimensional characters for the project. A modified marketplace is encompassed in the smart contract, which helps in basic buying, bidding, and completing different transactions. The owners get an additional asset bundle that contains a full 3D model that they might utilize to reduce and animate their Meebit.

## Rarible

It is one of the most prevalent Ethereum-based NFT markets, consenting users to create, sell, and buy NFT artwork and all the other types of collectibles.

The platform presented a new procedure of minting NFTs in October of the year 2021. The buyer pays the charges rather than the creator when the NFT is uploaded and both parties will relish the profits at the end.

# 4.2 Upcoming initiatives

Daily, more and more NFTs are being released. For 2022, the experts have predicted the following products to take centre stage.

## Space Runners

It is a digital sneaker company that launches handcrafted NFT assets in collaboration with celebrities and enterprises.

## Cool Kittens & Cats

It is a collection of 7,777 NFTs involving tiger-based characters on the Ethereum-based blockchain to help animal rescue. The project will comprise a questing system that will let holders complete a quest in exchange for a 50% royalty benefit.

In 2021, the NFT business reached its highest potential, considering digital gaming, artwork, and the possibility of owning and using digital land. There are a variety of projects that offer outstanding investment options, or you can just obtain NFTs devoted to digital artwork to add to your gathering of the most cutting-edge and ground-breaking works of art. Whatever your concerns are, NFTs are expected to have something for you. The good news is that novel projects are endlessly coming out and attracting the attention of the entire crypto community. For the future, just go through the potential success stories involving NFTs.

## Decentralization

It is the most notable project on our list. It is a metaverse project that profoundly relies on NFTs. Decentraland offers a simulated environment made up of unique pieces of land that you may buy and own by getting your hands on a corresponding NFT. Each piece of land offers the likelihood of starting a corporate, evolving game and software or even becoming the host of virtual events. The project has been creating the hype for a while, but it debuted too soon to store extensive attention.

**Doodles**

It is a bright NFT scheme with 10,000 generative NFTs by different artists Scott Martin, Evan Keast and Jordan Castro. They were also among the developers who assisted in the launch of CryptoKitties in 2017, the firstborn and most renowned NFT project in crypto history.

Scott Martin produced hundreds of dissimilar aesthetic characteristics for the collection, displayed in their new mission. Faced with irresistible demand, the project lastly tracked the path of many other NFT projects, combining the discrete characteristics to generate new art pieces by mixing them at random. Different NFTs have changing degrees of scarcity, judged by their features.

**MekaVerse**

It is a prevalent non-fungible token assortment based on Ethereum. This one has Mekas, which are robot-style artworks as NFTs. It comprises a total of 8,888 NFTs in the collection. The project has risen in admiration, garnering followers from worldwide.

With the NFT industry thriving, there is an overabundance of options for buying digital art, virtual land and gaming characters apart from multiple more options. The trends show that it is only a matter of time before we see the NFTs being more prevalent around us than ever.

## 4.3 NFTs & Celebrity Trends

The 2021 upsurge in the popularity of NFTs and crypto has enhanced the attention of everyone, including the world-known celebrities, who are minting their own NFTs and accepting sponsorship from crypto tokens. While NFTs are expected to remain popular, token authorizations will become outdated as the market gets more precise.

The general public's big wave of interest squeezed the cryptocurrency field in late 2020 and early 2021. The mainstream of this fad was engrossed in NFTs, which practiced a dramatic rise in admiration, resulting in the making of frequent artworks, photographs and trading cards. Every developer fantasized that their NFT would be one of the fortunate few to be sold for millions of dollars.

Snoop Dogg, Lindsay Lohan and Rob Gronkowski are among the celebs who have planned their own NFTs, which were traded for thousands of dollars each. This is a big step in the forward direction for the bitcoin field, as anything related to crypto is finally breaking through the mainstream.

Even though many people see celebrity NFTs as a barefaced cash grab, they are advantageous to crypto and blockchain in general, and they are not going away anytime soon.

Celebrities will endure being connected with NFTs for various reasons, one of which is the possible reward. A typical NFT on Ethereum costs a dollar or two to generate but may bring celebrity hundreds of thousands of dollars. For these people, such profit margins are unheard of, as they may make as much money from a single NFT sale as they would from an album or movie release. Celebrities and their managers will continue to gain the benefits as long as their profits surpass the cost of minting.

Additionally, as NFT marketplaces have grown in admiration, millions of users have begun moving towards crypto to purchase NFTs from their preferred celebrities. All they need is to obtain Ethereum, make a MetaMask account, and interrelate with smart contracts as part of the process. They are now part of the DeFi network, whether they recognize it or not, and will finally find their way into other decentralized applications.

Another reason for celebrity NFTs' unceasing popularity is their elegance, freshness, and a cool factor in the public's eyes. For instance, Baseball athlete Justin Turner donated a free NFT to every fan designated for him to play in the all-star. It shows that the interest of the common public and celebrities for the NFTs will only get enhanced with each passing day.

### Shawn Yue Man-lok

He is a Hong Kong-based actor and came to the NFT industry for the first time after getting partnered with Christie's. The former model gathered a personal collection, which he traded in September 2021. NFT items from Cryptopunks, Bored Ape Yacht Club and Meebits were among the most desirable in the collection.

### Justin Bieber

If you have been following Justin Bieber on social media, especially Instagram, you will have an idea about his interest and love for the NFTs. Bieber showed his liking for the various colorful bear images. Other celebrities, including Snoop Dogg and Tom Holland, also acclaimed the recently released collection of 10,111 photographs.

**Steph Curry**

Steph Curry is one of the biggest names in NBA history and he released a collection of more than 2500 NFTs, each costing US$333 on average. His collection includes digital copies of shoe products, which display the same pairs he had worn during his marvelous on-court accomplishments. The fans can use and show them off across multiple metaverses and virtual gaming worlds, even though the collection has already been sold out.

**Jimmy Fallon**

He is the host of the Tonight Show and has been a long-time associate of the NFT family. Fallon shared the latest addition to his gathering, a plain Bored Ape dressed in a sailor's costume. The NFT was bought for a little around $225,000.

**Snoop Dogg**

Snoop Dogg arrived in the NFT sector with an exhibition of his "A Journey with the Dogg" collection. The album is predicted to take listeners through the rapper's life and affectionate memories. It also includes quotes and photos by the singer.

## 4.3 Top-Rated & Well-Known NFTs

Because NFTs are highly exclusive, they are expensive. Traditional artwork was appreciated since it was the only version available, but digital art is much calmer to copy and re-form. NFTs, tokenize the art so that the owner can sell a certificate of ownership that verifies the asset's authenticity.

**The First Tweet**

"Just setting up my twttr," is the most popular tweet ever and the CEO himself was writing it. Jack Dorsey donated $2.9 million to charity by auctioning the tweet. A Malaysian buyer procured the tweet using the ether cryptocurrency.

**Hashmasks**

It is a living art collection formed by over 70 artists worldwide. It comprises 16,300 individual digital representations. Over three days, one of the items made a 100,000 % profit.

**Doge NFT**

The infamous dog Kabosu encouraged the creation of the cryptocurrency dogecoin. It is the original 'Doge' meme from 2010. PleasrDAO bought the NFT and currently sells slight ownership of it, meaning that anyone can own a dollar worth of the NFT.

**Grime**

Grimes traded a total of ten pieces, the most popular of which was an exclusive film called 'Death of the Old.' Two more pieces, Mars and Earth, each with multiple copies, attracted $7,500 per copy before sales ended.

## 4.4 Brand value with NFT

The internet is full of multiple examples of corporations using NFTs to highlight the names of their brands. To have an idea, read about some top-ranked names in this regard.

**NFTacoBell**

It is known for its infrequently risky digital marketing stunts. It put out 25 NFTs to honor the return of potatoes to their menu earlier in the year 2022.

Consequently, they were the first fast-food corporation to squeeze the NFT movement. All NFTs were traded within 30 minutes, with one of them selling for as much as $3500 and being resold for as much as 10 ETH. Additionally, the brand declared that all incomes from the original sale and income collected from resales would go toward its Scholarship program.

**ASICS**

Asics similar to TacoBell was the first name in their industry to go on the NFT bandwagon. Their Sunrise Red campaign began in July of the year 2021 and featured multiple limited-edition digital sneakers as well as several other products up for auction.

However, the brand's goal was not to benefit from the promotion right away. Asics said that the NFTs were the first step toward a future where virtual goods endorse physical exercise. To support the artists who produced the NFTs, the entire campaign's profits were put in the ASICS, a charity residence program.

The company also made it clear that they were aware of the operation's environmental influence and acquiring carbon credits to offset the emissions.

**Robert Mondavi NFT Collection**

Robert Mondavi has teamed up with Bernardaud, a French luxury porcelain firm, to develop a limited series of porcelain wines bottles.

An NFT, made by artist Clay Heaton, is linked to each of the wine bottles to authenticate its origin and genuineness and serve as documentation of ownership. Individuals will get their bottles from the enterprise that are linked with the NFTs.

**What NFTs Mean for Marketing's Future**

The examples mentioned above are just a few of the many ways that organizations, corporations and artists are embracing the NFT movement. Multiple brands have a whole new advertising field thanks to NFTs. This assists them in coming up with novel and innovative approaches to involve their fans, increase brand exposure, and produce new revenue streams.

NFTs are a win-win situation for both companies and consumers, letting the latter own a dynamic piece of an asset that is not one of its products and sell back at a profit if anticipated.

Of course, the environmental influence of NFTs is a chief consideration, and marketers will need to figure out how to strike a balance between the trend and its implications. Given the high demand for tokens, more environmentally friendly methods of producing tokens are likely to emerge soon.

# Conclusion

It turns out that NFTs are here to stay for a longer period as the trends show that these are bringing in huge revenue generation for all the interested people. It does not matter whether you are interested in the NFT-based games or not. You can have entertainment and profits from the games if you are into video gaming, but you can also start looking for an alternative if you do not like games much. Now you can go out to a perfect platform to buy a virtual piece of land at a virtual place. It will be done easily with the help of ETH currency and NFTs. Speaking of other ways to mint money through NFTs, you can also focus on other domains like video making photography and even the sports industry has some notable opportunities.

In any case, the sole aim should be to go for the unique products in nature so that they might have the attention of the customers. The greater the rarity, the greater will be the number of people interested in your NFTs. Start thinking about this beneficial domain as it holds a huge potential and promises greater profits for everyone. Suppose you find it hard to get an idea about its potential significance and growth potentials. In that case, you need to go through the ongoing celebrity and technological trends in this book.

Consequently, you will have all the understanding that is necessary for a perfect investment in the NFT domain. You will be able to locate the most reputable NFT platforms for buying and selling of the non-fungible tokens. Moreover, detailed insights about the top NFT projects will give you an idea about which domains to prefer and which ones to ignore.

www.ingramcontent.com/pod-product-compliance
Lightning Source LLC
Chambersburg PA
CBHW071517210326
41597CB00018B/2793